House of Jars
Poems

Hester L. Furey

Frayed Edge Press
Philadelphia, PA

Copyright 2024, Hester L. Furey

Published by Frayed Edge Press in 2024

Frayed Edge Press
Philadelphia, PA

http://frayededgepress.com

Cover illustration by Lente Scura
www.lentescura.net

Author photo by Bill Roa

Library of Congress Control Number: 2024949912

Publisher's Cataloging-in-Publication Data

Names: Furey, Hester Lee.
Title: House of jars : poems / Hester L. Furey.
Description: Philadelphia, PA : Frayed Edge Press, 2024.
Identifiers: LCCN 2024949912 | ISBN 9781642510591 (pbk.) | ISBN 9781642510607 (EPUB) | ISBN 9781642510614 (Kindle) | ISBN 9781642510621 (iBook)
Subjects: LCSH: American poetry – 21st century. | Mental health—Poetry. | Menopause – Poetry. | Physicians – Poetry. | Reality – Poetry. | BISAC: POETRY / American / General. | POETRY / Women Authors. | POETRY / Subjects & Themes / Death, Grief, Loss.
Classification: LCC PS3606.U748 H68 2024 | DDC 813 M67--dc23
LC record available at https://lccn.loc.gov/2024949912

Table of Contents

Acknowledgments	iii
Preface	v
Recipe for Star Bread	1
Flight	2
Eleven Years	5
Retreat	7
House of Jars	8
Reynoldstown Cat Races	9
Susu Watari	11
Sycamore, Georgia, December 2015	13
Gone Buggy	15
Moderns and Their Bugs	
A Doctor Visit	18
Baby in Baltimore	20
Three Theories of Art	23
Dog Days in Santa Fe, 1925	25
Bug Relativism	28
Moderns and Mosquitoes	30
Conjuring Moses	
Freud	35
Jump at the Sun	38
People of the Sun	40
El Norte	42
Moses, Man of the Mountain	45

Building the Diamond Body
- What's Bugging Her ... 50
- Broken Landings ... 52
- Ancestors Come to Greet Us ... 53
- Building the Diamond Body ... 55
- After the Ex ... 58
- Salve, Spider ... 59
- Sentinel ... 60
- Strange Angels ... 62
- Young William James ... 67
- The Cut ... 69

Notes ... 71

About the Author ... 73

Acknowledgments

"After the Ex" appeared in *The Wise Owl*, Flamingo Issue, March 2024.

"Broken Landings" appeared in *Last Leaves*, Issue 3 October 31, 2021.

"Baby in Baltimore" appeared in *Blue Mountain Review*, February 2021.

"Dog Days in Santa Fe, 1925" appeared in the Georgia Poetry Society's annual anthology, *The Reach of Song*, 2020.

"A Doctor Visit," "Bug Relativism," and "Moderns and Mosquitoes" appeared in *Blue Mountain Review*'s July 2019, October 2019, and January 2020 issues.

"Three Theories of Art" appeared in *Eyedrum Periodically*. The Art Issue, Fall 2017.

"What's Bugging Her" appeared in *Eyedrum Periodically*. Marginal Creatures Issue, Spring 2017.

"House of Jars" appeared in *Eyedrum Periodically*. Alchemy Issue, Winter 2016.

With deepest gratitude to those who led, carried, and healed me:

Franklin Abbott, the Adda sisters, Catherine Adunni, Penney Balmes, Sherry Barren, Glenn Baughman, Linda Baughman, Elizabeth Bazen, Linda Berggren, Pam Blum, Ian Boccio, Suzy Borden, Michael Brün, Paul Buhle, Yoganand Michael Carroll, Meg Carter, Cathy Clark, Windy Cooler, Steve Davenport, Will Griffin, John Glaze, Margo Gomes, Paula Greene, Emily Gretz, Jacci Gruninger, Richard Haight, Ed Hall, Misty Harper, Cindy Hayes, Bob Helms, Cinqué Hicks, Paige Hood, William Hufschmidt, Stephanie Kohler, Leon Lashner, John Laughinghawk, Alicia Bay Laurel, Usha Laxmi, Jennifer Wen Ma, Leah Maines, Duane Marcus, Debra Mazer, Michele Moody, Patricia Mulligan, Cary Nelson, Miriam Payton, Jennifer Proctor, Kim Reimann, Pat Rich, Jade Rivers, Aaron Ruscetta, Priscilla Smith, Christina Springer, Dr. Aaron Sui, Althea Sumpter, Susan Thurman, Amanda Trevelino, Maria Trotter, Justin Waters, Rhett and Richard Watson.

Special thanks to ART PAPERS, the Halsey Museum at College of Charleston, the Library of Congress, the Lillian E. Smith Center, Vassar College, and always and forever, Pranakriya School of Yoga Healing Arts

Preface

For years I have carried around with me a quotation from Margaret Atwood's novel *The Handmaid's Tale*: "In reduced circumstances you have to believe all kinds of things.... The desire to live attaches itself to strange objects."

House of Jars weaves together three sequences of poems: the journey of a character called Skeleton Woman through a mental health crisis based on my own experience of menopause; the stories of her pantheon of modernist doctor-writers whose own mental health crises changed their writing; and Conjuring Moses, which can only be characterized as a morality tale about the power and danger of esoteric quests and the frailty of human knowledge.

A yogic journey, an examination of attachments, unites the three strands of development. The book dwells on the experience of not knowing what is real, of living a long time with a version of reality that is not easy to verify but still occupies a lot of psychic real estate. That experience can be both frightening and exhilarating. Maybe the heart of the book is the poem "Three Theories of Art," which takes inspiration from Elizabeth Grosz's *Chaos, Territory, Art*; namely, the idea that art depends upon a deliberate setting aside of dependence on structure, a willing engagement with chaos. The generative force then transmits to others through a temporary frame such as a book or painting.

This work began as an experiment. Prior to the fall of 2015 I had always carefully kept my poetry separate from my archivally based academic work in literary history. Then, during the five years that elapsed between quitting one full-time academic job and finding another, I developed a new understanding of modernist literary history that I felt could only be expressed in poetry rather than the conventional essay for an academic journal. Whereas the 19th century barreled along on the strength of great beliefs and -isms, the 20th century has propelled itself forward by a combination of technocracy and disillusionment. This idea is well established. But I wanted a way to preserve overlooked nuances of 20th century human experience.

Beginning with *The Autobiography of William Carlos Williams*, I began to follow the accounts of many modernists who had insect-borne illnesses or mental health crises provoked by insect encounters. Very little conventional literary criticism has addressed the role of such moments of passage in creative development of these or any other writers. To develop these poems, I traveled to the Margaret Mead Papers at Library of Congress twice and the Ruth Benedict Papers at Vassar. The pandemic shutdown prevented further visits to archives, so I expanded my accounts of modernist crisis to include stories of writers such as Gertrude Stein, who panicked after medical student peers pranked her by pouring glucose into her urine and most likely tampered with her blood specimen as well. I added the story of Rachel Carson, who faced the task, while privately struggling with breast cancer, of explaining to her entire society that DDT was far from a godsend. Somewhere along the way I realized that Freud and Zora Neale Hurston had published books on Moses in 1939, and I began to follow that thread. Then the Moses cycle, which turned out to include Robert Oppenheimer, burst into the center of the book. After reading an account of an insect-plagued journey to Brazil from 1865, I included a piece on William James that reaffirms the theoretical underpinning of it all: the centrality of doubt in any attempt at knowledge, a pragmatic willingness both to consider and to set aside belief, and openness to the generative power of chance.

"Art and science do not establish themselves despite failure but through it.... It is useful for the man of action to find out under what conditions his undertakings are valid."—Simone de Beauvoir, *The Ethics of Ambiguity*

"I want to share with you this wilderness of failure. The others have built you a highway—fast lanes in both directions. I offer you a journey without direction, uncertainty and no sweet conclusion. When the light faded, I went in search of myself. There were many paths and many destinations."—Derek Jarman, *The Garden*

"Let one *omer* of it be kept throughout the ages, in order that they may see the bread that I fed you in the wilderness when I brought you out from the land of Egypt. And Moses said to Aaron, 'Take a jar, put one *omer* of manna in it, and place it before Adonai, to be kept throughout the ages.'"—Exodus 16: 32-34

Recipe for Star Bread

On a cross-town bus, a character from Dr. Seuss
makes ready for plant rescue at a place she once called home.
She seems placid enough, this goofy grandma.
Fresh from a trip down the crazy river,
where she hopped from rock to rock,
sometimes wading, other times
giving up and floating, she gives thanks
that the territory was not altogether unfamiliar,
that she could return. Under the patchwork blue hat,
behind the parti-colored readers, a poem leavens.
Still lumpy and sticky, but she can feel it growing,
smells with satisfaction the fermenting agent at work:
a love triangle of modernist doctor-poets.
Their pain and confusion, struggles with attachment,
the mismatch of love and inadequacy of story-houses
give birth to discovery, books and hypotheses,
schools of thought, whole disciplines of study.
"He put her in a pumpkin shell, and there he kept her very well."
She will have to bring her shovel home on the bus.
Oh, she is at home with the stares. The day before,
she cried and rubbed dirt on her face.
Maybe today will be better. It must be done.
She thinks of Ruth Benedict among the Zuni,
driven to her roof in Cochiti by bedbugs and, no doubt,
the aggravation of that "miserable child" on her way
to Samoa. The poetry of accident in our married names.
The necessary schizophrenia of partly deaf interpreters,
wariness of narrators and informants, on one hand, and
friends who protect you in your mourning
and promise to construct bee hotels,
the long unbreakable loves that hide in history
until a reader comes who can receive them,
someone who can digest star bread.

Flight

First she left
her man, the job,
then her house, then
a lot of stories about her
future. Flinging
one
after another
out the window,
watching
the brittle things
bounce and
break
in the streets below.
New meaning arose there,
hovered just out of reach
over shards and fragments,
a kind of scrying.
Must be a term for it—
Schizomancy?
Fissure vision?
Around her, so many shaking
heads, so many questions
revealed her real friends.

Changing course, cloaked
in the unlikely matriarchal blessing
she turned south and east,
traveled into the autumnal sun.
A week on the coast
before the money ran out
seemed the best medicine:
beginning with

a night in a bunkhouse
in the reeking marsh,
sleepless among the forest hippies,
who snored or swore.
She laughed with another woman.
Welcome to our world, motherfucker.
Front porch homies cajoled,
a chanting morning in their glass bowl
to blast the headache away,
and on to St. Simon's,
an isle of the blessed,
for Meg and healing sands
that never failed her, the windy
winding canopied streets,
the oldest trees she's ever seen.
A clouded over full moon night,
a cruise with the riverkeeper.
Coming back,
they let her stand up front,
high on the air and spray,
reciting her heretic's mantra:
verweile doch. Du bist so schön.

In Savannah, libraries and cemeteries,
Crystal Eastman theses
and resurrection ferns.
Soaking in all the medicine now,
finally taking time
to begin to heal, to know
what that might mean.
Back home on the porch,
giving thanks to the land
that held her these years,
Skelly rests her cheek on the floor.

"Sometimes the Lord only
lets you see just so far,"
the matriarch said.
She had poured that tea down
her face so casually,
recited the psalms
so surely, no fear.
Now the moon's bright boat,
grown slimmer, sails into darkness.
Her insides shift,
losing ballast, going instar,
making ready for lift off.

Eleven Years

"Ek Ong Kar, Sat Guru Prasad, Sat Guru Prasad, Ek Ong Kar"

White Tantric clears out in a day
"eleven years of unconscious crap"—
so the kundalini kids promise.
She bought the ticket, prepared
the pupal wrappings and,
expecting to sleep on the floor,
carpooled to an ashram in Knoxville,
but instead was floored by luxury,
waking to dawn song, the wild
new friends, the old women
with their tales of Yogi-Ji, how they came
in the 1970s to build these places
where their children still live,
the sudden longing to connect
flaring up in her misanthrope heart.
Forty days later she moved house.

Now, months past, life turned
upside down in a good way,
she sees she had to take
the batshit express, could never
have reasoned her way here.
Fresh from a first-class lesson in how
abundance can be bad, she
is writing again. She sleeps, often,
not grinding her teeth. Still
broke, nothing new to tell, and
creditors going crazy, but they
are like Prince's mother.
What she wonders, living sweet
slow days the like of which she

hasn't seen since early high school, is
which eleven years? Eleven continuous
years, or eleven total? And the blocks
of crap—are they solid or composites?
We talking cherry-picked crap?
Or crap particles, maybe only the largest
get sifted out, or pressed together,
like toxic psychic particle board.
Her sun-flooded room seems
haunted by the seventies, seeds
her mind each morning with songs
all but forgotten.

Retreat

At the yoga retreat in the mountains,
old ones nurse their knees, trade tales.
Skeleton Woman confesses
an addiction to Tiger Balm.
Martha says she first heard of it
in Kathmandu, kids hawking it
in the streets—and she thought
it must be a code, a kind of pot.
The quiet one has brought
an infrared heating pad.
They take turns napping on it.

Panic-vacuuming has wrecked an elbow.
The dominant hand slow to release
from its pointless grasping, thumb numb,
prickly at best. They call this trigger finger,
a mudra if done by choice. Maurice
says her hard-working hand
has gone on strike.
The beautiful young spirit healer
says she smells like his grandmother,
and she roars with laughter.
What a sweet talker he is.
It's true. She doesn't care.
Ulnar nerve possibly damaged,
grief-scoured into a blank presence,
sleepless without the smelly salve,
she awaits a new telos, living only
to fight another day.

House of Jars

Home from the mycelium wars,
I strip, bathe, wash every conceivable surface.
My life fits between the washer and the dryer.
I know I can't go on like this.
When plants (and maybe animals—that is my theory)
begin to die, they throw all their energy to seed.
My tree uprooted, I came here
to survive, but did I? The jury's out.
What is left of what I was?
Will anything that I call me live on?
It has no juice of a new life, if it is one.
While I wait for marching orders,
all must be lint-rolled, soaked in tea-tree oil,
dried twice, thrown away or preserved.
I am scraping bottom, another container
of light and air, agnostic,
here in the house of jars.

Reynoldstown Cat Races

Reynoldstown cat races begin at dawn.
Doo dah, doo dah. Song ghosts bounce
footpads along: bah dum pah dum
pah dum pah dump. The one thing they approve,
the thirty-foot midsection of this lawnless
city shotgun house between the front door and
the plumbed addition. One cat's prison, another's refuge.

Pulling the mala from under the pillow, she
recalls her mother's easy laughing unkind mind,
the unneighborly mockery of a fresher hillbilly family,
how they mispronounced words: "bolla" for bottle,
"pulla" for puddle. Then begins to tell the 108 beads.
Om dum durgaiye namaha. All, however they spoke,
whatever books they did or didn't read, lived in these houses.

Mala/mallow—she had to leave behind the althea,
a clone from PawPaw's bush. He called it "alfea" (a Cockney
in the woodshed?). On the porch one survivor preserves
the memory of the ass-numbing dining room chairs.
In Mrs. Butler's living room, made her entire home now,
on an abandoned set of *Gone with the Wind*
as read in childhood before travel, she breathes.

Can't expect everyone to know Latin. Soon the sun
will pour in, turn the felines languid and purry just as
she must leave. At present all is percussion and discord.
Outside her door now echoing yowls fill the hall;
a toy snake is dying a terrible death.
The tiny kitten they call Badger, wildly
happy, running with the cool cats.

They should call her Mouse, a creature small and gray,
but also a sly joke the kids didn't get. Nursing hands
covered with bites from the razor teeth, she left it at
"read Walter Mosley." The sky lightens as she prays.
There are many worlds. None of us can see them all.
Om dum durgaiye namaha.
Bah dum pah dum pah dum pah dump.

Susu Watari

The belligerent pacifist with a voice like a dj
says he never understood that film,
when she tells him she has blundered
into a crossroads of the spirits, is doing some time.
They laugh, and she doesn't tell him
about the soot, her daily battles with bugs,
how very often other signals can't get through.
It would just confuse him.
He says he couldn't identify the pattern,
the randomness of the gods beyond him.
Soberly she nods. Yes, that's how they roll.

The forced, false gardens of city dwellers make her sad.
Her room is a goldfish bowl, night-lit
by street lamps and porches of nervous neighbors.
The insomniac rail yard emits at all hours wails,
minor chords, beeping perseverations, protracted groans,
while she sleeps like a child. She loses days
but gains worlds. Her mother told stories
of old people picking at something only they saw
in the bed clothes. She knows the legends
of the soot spirits appearing to those near death.
Undaunted, she prays *ho'oponopono*

to the mushrooms and the small bugs
that eat them, saying: very well, you did your job.
You drove me from my home in the woods.
I'm not mad at you though many think me mad.
I forgive you. I love you. Thank you. Forgive me. Let me go.
Some days she wakes and hears the old house
singing to itself. She cares for the children,
never misses a day of work. Long ago
she made her peace with being invisible.

Now it cloaks her, protects her. Few
see her trials, and that is for the best.

Her body feels well again. The madness
brings a longed-for clarity and new writing.
The many losses appear small from this side
of the ledger. Harder to explain
what she got in the exchange; having combed
a collection of words like ocean-scrap,
unspeakable, no less real. She handles
the rationalists like any other believers,
gently. Fragile creatures, their pristine
snow globe worlds maintained with care,
no room for the shadows she bears.

Sycamore, Georgia December 2015

At the big magnolia out front, a whisper,
"do you remember me?" barely breathing,
against the chance any nosing neighbors might hear.
Somewhere along here I took first steps,
learned awareness; voices and histories
unfurled sweetly inside my brain.
Through the fence just visible,
the grape arbor, absorbed by tanglewood.
The sandy fens behind the abandoned orchard
a reminder of what it all used to be.

This is what happens to the houses of the poor:
tin roofs rust, curl at the corners to admit
rodents and birds, outbuildings fill with junk,
microbes and spores creep up through wooden floors.
Mold slowly restores the building to its elements.
Someone tore off the sweet airy porches, long ago.
Paint peels, vines and moss climb walls,
pull down chimneys. Fish ponds vanish.
Only the trees preserve the old magic, and there,
on the corner, live the narcissi where she taught me
about the beautiful boy and the sad nymph.

My flights here always laden with an agenda,
the first item, perpetually deferred: "don't go crazy."
This time, also, "computer—can it be salvaged?"
and "make my cousin walk around the block."
The holy calm incites a terrible longing and equal fear.
I tax my kinfolks' patience, intruding on their comfort
with molotov values and talk of other worlds.
I threw her rocking chair out this year, had to—
it grew moldy. That and much else I haven't told them.
Fungi create strange economies, change what's real.

Wood sorrel clusters have spread all over the yard.
A cloud of buzzards hangs beyond the horse farm.
Most of the feeling has returned to my hand.
Just now jacket weather, a week before Christmas,
many fields of cotton yet unharvested.
A few miles east of Eisenhower's autobahn
brown signs mark Jeff Davis's last hiding place.
The afternoon's past its zenith. Bored cats and dogs stare
discontent at the stranger who walks their streets
feeling for phantom roots, talking to the trees.

Gone Buggy

The gentle anarchist leaves his car,
tickles her with "now don't go to Alabama"—
as if she would. She isn't that far gone.
He says the bugs have gotten into her mind.
Not that they're not real, which is kind.
The doctor sister gives poison salve.
Skelly coats herself in it from head to toe
twice. The herbalist ladies give formitin
and bug-bits to eat, urging,
"they'll leave you if you become one."
Becoming insect: a pale, shaking ghost
cleans, irons, examines all minutely,
tries to get a grip, a mysophobic mess,
trailing flakes, beliefs, and possessions.
Fearful of survival, in equal parts for and against,
an unsettled balance, the self steadied
in sequences of repetitive motions
of often inconsequential purpose, no focus.
The tiny pills pop floral under the tongue.
She sets fire to another small pile of sage.
Storm mother, I come walking in your path.
Protect me. Let me pass through these woods.

Moderns and Their Bugs

A Doctor Visit

Having wished once for time travel, laying
a board across her chair to write like Woolf,
Skeleton Woman reads with interest now
stories of the moderns and their bug-wars.
A once handsome doctor-poet, he of the red wheelbarrow,
the giant number 5, the stolen plums, arrests her with tales
of interning at the French hospital, New York, where
"as at all hospitals the battle against vermin went on endlessly."
The German lab chief, aka "the Wrath of God," rages:
roaches lick the slides clean every night,
the diseased blood a delicious snack.
The intern, a college pal of Ezra Pound,
joins him in a night raid. "Hundreds" cover
every surface, revealed by flashlights. In an orgy
of ether deaths, the chief's delight "savage,"
but "the job," the older poet says, "was hopeless."

At the Nursery and Child's Hospital in Hell's Kitchen,
his patients mostly abandoned children, or tenement
dwellers, who suffer the epidemics Malthus
considered "natural" population control for the poor.
The delivery room manager, a gal with a grill, wise cracks
that the building needs a 3-foot banner wrap around:

> BABIES FRESH
> EVERY HOUR,
> ANY COLOR DESIRED,
> 100% ILLEGITIMATE.

A rich patron offers her apartment on Riverside,
a convalescent home for those guaranteed not to die.
A bug stealthier than roaches, infectious gastro-enteritis.
All are dead within five days.

The doctor confesses to taping a crying toddler's mouth.
Once. Then knowing somehow in that moment
why the babies wouldn't settle, removing the adhesive:
bedbugs. Confirming the theory with a test, he buys
half a barrel of sulfur chunks, builds fires
throughout the wards, sealing windows and doors,
excepting only the exit, where he receives every child naked,
wrapping each in sterile cloth. Used bedding
left inside. When all, stripped, have been removed,
he goes back, lights alcohol fires, diving out
just ahead of the flash, seals the door behind him.
The next day nurses sweep out "pyramids" of bugs.
The doctor as exterminator, a multi-valent trope.

Back home in New Jersey, obstetrician to Guinea Hill,
after night births among the friendly Italians,
the young doctor-poet can neither sleep nor type poems
until he has removed his clothes in the tub. Even then,
once inside his straw hat's sweatband he finds a bed bug
a day later, the size of a lentil, fat with blood.

Baby in Baltimore

Baby bade an early goodbye to
a girly good buy, to
the letter of the law, to
the senses of sentences. Baby,
our lady of the roses and bellies.
Between May and Mabel,
between Leo and Leon,
William and Henry, and
then Leo and Alice:
building triangles and boxes in verse
and prose. Mother and Father gone,
always Baby. Holding to shreds
and shredding patriarchal poetry,
the homesick expatriate, leaving
behind the looming dismal fathers:
"Alas for an unbuttered influence say I."

Baby followed Leo to Harvard,
became the pet of William James.
Thence to Woods Hole for embryology,
finally to Johns Hopkins, where,
between Barker and Bull,
spiked piss in the lab,
likely sabotaged slides of blood:
they hazed her out of medical school.
Fat—Jewish—woman—"flopping"—
Baby wore no corset and "didn't give a damn."
So they said, but she did.
They made her dissect
baby brain after baby brain.
A brain is a brain is a brain
unless it's not.

House of Jars

Rotations in the labor wards
of black Baltimore, so she
knew well where the bodies came from.
After the blood incident Baby hired
a welterweight to box with her.

Later the famous art collector and poet
claimed only "boredom" as the spur
of departure, but in her notebooks
remembered being sick in the yard
after exams. She had written off
being observant but could not quite yet
shake the woman part, floppy as she was.
There beliefs more than body
held her back. Baby was
in love and writing about triangles,
about hidden compulsions,
perseverations, perversions,
developing her own ways
of studying the brain.

The professors gave her one last chance,
one last brain to model.
Fossilized demon voices in the archive:
"Can't you find a six months' infant for her?"
After sixty-three pages of drawings
and twenty-five pages of notes,
fashioning a "fuck you" in plaster
—her only known sculpture—
she sailed for Europe to study the roots
of modern English, to help poetry
escape the sentence. The jailbreak took
some time. The lost lives of underseam
Baltimore haunted her. She put *QED*

away for a while, likewise *Fernhurst*.
"Demonstrate" has a demon and a god in it.
By *Three Lives*, she hit her stride
rivaling her master, Cezanne.
Her brother made her a coral brooch.
Her pal Picasso painted her portrait.
Yet another troublesome Mabel made
a path-clearing to her growing fame
before the flowers of friendship faded.

Privately simply deciding to live as a man,
Baby married an odd little bird of a woman,
wrote weird book after weird book.
Cutting her hair, she adopted a look
somewhere between a monk
and a Chinese emperor. She
drove an ambulance in the war,
composed an opera in 1927 for an
all black cast; no other, not even
Verdi, had ever done it. To beat
back the blankness that arose after
a best-seller and American lectures,
Baby wrote a murder mystery,
revisiting how a corpse can be interesting.
Poet-soldiers named her "Marraine."
She named a generation, became
a face of Paris. Her will lists her place
of residence as Baltimore.

Three Theories of Art

"The words of a dead man / Are modified in the guts of the living."
—W.H. Auden, "In Memory of W.B. Yeats"

Skeleton Woman doesn't know how
the chancellor could say
"poetry makes nothing happen."
Bad poetry caused the Red Scares, the World Wars
—every war, come to that—chased her
across the country and back, packed up
her entire house, moved her into town
to a goldfish bowl in a shotgun house
four blocks from the train.
She believes three theories at once.
Poetry as a language that enables us
to process and possibly share inward life.
Art, as the anarchists said, the excrement
of process. A fossil record of emotion once present.
Or, as Grosz said, generative chaos, the angel
we must wrestle; structure the demon who tempts.
Worming their way into our psyches, they
perform magic dances of presence and absence,
annoy and obsess, wreck our lives and bore
our friends until we place temporary frames
on them, send them back out into the world,
whence they escape, if all goes well, moving
on to the next person. Trickster made this place.
We never know how it will go.
Rosalind Krauss can move to storage now.
Escape, to lose a cape. Collegio, a hooded man.
A scape is the green stalk a garlic puts up.
Arguments about whether to pinch it.

Scott Nearing and the Eastmans said
they escaped wealth.
Maybe that is what she has done.

Dog Days in Santa Fe, 1925

"O God, let me be awake—awake in my lifetime."—Ruth Benedict

In a total solar eclipse, New York City stock still
for ten minutes, no traffic, no phone calls, the year began:
unseen, old worlds splintered and spun out new ones;
angels and demons of progress streamed across the sky,
seeding projects and secrets, enmities and alliances. In spring,
New Mexico unfurled a red Zia sun on yellow, its new flag,
a beacon to civilization's mellower discontents.
In Manhattan, two married women quietly became lovers.
Another couple, Willie and Edith, left the city just ahead of them.
The Professor's House ran serially in summer issues of *Collier's*
while Willie rode around Santa Fe pursuing traces of her archbishop.
Ruth and Margaret stepped into the whirlwind in late July.
Around the globe *Mein Kampf* appeared on shelves, and
a black sun proliferated, portending another clash of empires.
Clarence Darrow, whose name was a poem, traveled
to Tennessee to oppose his old friend The Great Commoner,
shocked the court by calling the prosecutor as a witness,
whereupon Bryan won, then died. But the lovers lived oblivious;
all the joy and ruses of summer, getting to that train,
their sole focus a few days together with no dissembling,
of nights lying breast to breast. After Chicago, conductors
set fine screens in the windows so the sweet prairie air
and waxing moonlight poured in, mixed with lovers' whispers.
In the high plains they passed into the old invaders' trail,
the air growing cooler as they rose, rolling through the mountains
before the slipstream sent them different ways
at the start of August, just outside the Grand Canyon.

Ruth followed the railroad back, retraced their route
before turning south under a full moon. In Cochiti, with bedbugs
for spirit guides, she climbed onto the roof each night
and flew like a witch in the dark. Not here to save a dying culture—
no one could do that, and truth be told, even she was a miner of sorts—
here to find her own lost country, become one of the gods,
answer her own prayer. The night sky pushed her back
into herself, then exalted her into an unnameable future,
the promised reunion in Rome, stories of lovers separated
by the Milky Way but brought back together by cycles
sure as the tides and spheres. With visions of her beloved's body,
fate-bound and nauseated, on a ship crossing the Pacific,
she sent her spirit out across the water, a guardian
to the younger woman, becoming the cradling vessel.
As the moon waned and Earth whirled through the Perseids,
her wishes streaked out to meet every piece of burning debris.
Sleep could wait; it was all worth it, her heart equal to the strain.
Some days she watched Sirius rise before dawn—a rainbow star—
Aborigines called it the sun's winter wife. Many times
brighter, it lives in hiding behind our day's smaller light.
She would always be a fox among the hedgehogs.

Under harsh noon rays she sat with old Nick,
her informant. With little patience for her questions,
he placed in her palm a crystal from a copper mine,
a malachite worn smooth with rubbing.
What do you see? he asked. Turning it over,
she found on one side people assembled in a canyon
on the banks of a sacred river. On the other,
a ship in sail under a night sky. When inverted,
it revealed a tree of life under two suns
and a shadow that drove people into caves.
She wrote to Margaret of the Jemez mountains:

"When I am God, I'm going to build my city there."
Up the fault line, in the Valles Caldera,
the laughing Oppenheimer boys raced their horses
like madmen, pursued by deerflies.

Bug Relativism

"So it appears that . . ., the African men of magic found out the deadly qualities of graveyard dirt. In some way they discovered that the earth surrounding a corpse that had sufficient time to thoroughly decay was impregnated with deadly power. It might, in some accidental way, come out of the ancestor worship of West Africa."—Zora Neale Hurston, *Tell My Horse*

"Belief in magic is older than writing,"
says Papa Franz's daughter, a storm queen,
lightning painted across and down her back.
A born anthropologist, lover of the crossroads
and those who crossed them, she rolled her birthday forward
ten years, then drove south in a Chevrolet,
to phosphate mines, lumber and turpentine camps,
posing as a bootlegger, collecting stories and songs,
shreds of African survivals, holding her own cards close,
and taking the temperature for hoodoo in each town.

In the Panhandle chiggers, mosquitoes, gnats, and boll weevils
peppered her "lying contests." She feared no damn bugs,
been walking into other folks' camps and looking around
since she was a child; knives were a different matter.
Undeterred by tales of subcutaneous scorpions and spiders,
seeking out
every root doctor in New Orleans, humbling herself time after time,
asking to be a student. Isolated and naked,
fasting and seeing visions for three days,
finally crowned with snake skins, she
got her black cat bone the hard way.

Haitians remind her: the Africans had a god of disease.
Mosquitoes haunt the mangrove swamps of La Gonave

but she waxes Guggenheim-lyrical; "the moonlight tasted like wine."
There also lives Vixama, the volcano god "who sits with a hive
of honey-bees in his long flowing beard."
Surrounded by animal sacrifice, rumors of zombies,
physicians who long to know the secret drug, the maid Lucille
who cautions, "don't run to every drum you hear."
No mention of pests, in all that blood and rum on the ground,
but cannibal gangs, and microbe survivals in animal hair and graveyard dirt.

Visiting the white caretaker of the insane,
another "doctor," a Navy man gone native, she longs
to linger trading stories on his swinging porch beds, but
wakes the morning after a party to watch the day be born.

"It took shape out of a ropy white mist,   but there it was,
the very last day that God had made,
            and it went about the business of changing people
    the way days always do."

She has an abiding weakness for these white fathers—
the old cowboy who cut her cord, let her ride on his horse,
took her fishing, and told her not to be a nigger;
Papa Franz, her dear Carl. She makes up her mind to go home,
write a book about Moses the conjure man, but before she can,
in seven weeks, unable to stop, writes *Their Eyes were Watching God*.

Moderns and Mosquitoes

"The Sepik is the longest river no one has ever heard of."—Gordon White,
Star Ships: A Prehistory of the Spirits

At the crossroads of Gondwana and Laurasia,
mosquitoes married us.
The discontented former headhunters
looked sideways, receiving our gifts and payments.
To the end they insisted
their way was better. The Sepik
has no delta, but people have cultivated rice there
since before the Flood.

Now, looking at the blood work
and the myths, two markers date this place,
a viable candidate for a possible Eden/Atlantis:
three separate malarial gene adaptations;
and, more telling, a subterranean confluence of story
without parallel outside Australia and Africa,
of Crocodile swimming, world without end
(Gondwana)
and the mismatched and quarreling brothers—
murder, displacement, loss of home
(Laurasia).

They guard the origin hole with care,
keeping away the destructive Europeans,
lest we unmake all in our will to power.
We had always lived in Laurasia.
To us Orion had forever been a hunter
brought down by a scorpion,
his belt never wise men or women in a canoe,
bound for the Pleiades. We assumed

the tallest island on Earth had always been so,
not a continent, though we began
by going up a mountain. I was carried
in a sort of sack, with as little mind
to my comfort as if I were potatoes.
Without a brother to fight, Reo
had stripped me of my personhood,
battered me without remorse,
beaten a child out of me.

After two abortive forays into remote tribes,
we retreated to the river, to Bateson's netted tree.
An Englishman, Gregory topped our
pecking order, we colonials deferring,
almost by instinct, to big brother.

So he plucked me, wounded bird,
away from Reo, salving my many wounds,
feeding my starving mind, binding my lame ankle,
sending me sugar and quinine. Of course I loved him.
Ruth, our distant but ever present Pleiadean light,
had sent her manuscript, a kind of benediction on our gathering.

The air above the lake was black with mosquitoes.
Waiting out a village raid that never happened,
as Reo slept with his loaded Webbley, we
shared cigarettes in the dark and entered
a process of change, a conversation for the ages,
sorting human temperaments into
a Prussian cross, the four compass points
north, south, fey, and turk. I moved then
through deliria of love and malaria,
witnessed my first birth.
Reo joined a men's lodge,

partaking in a raid. When he returned
I secretly counted his unspent cartridges.
He always loved his sorcerers too much.
Unplanning, we reenacted the Laurasian triad
with a slight twist: Reo dismembered me,
said he did not see the tortoise upon which earth rests;
Gregory worked magic to bring me back
to myself. After a long ocean voyage, a separation
of years in which I wrote, "do you suppose that we
will ever have a house together anywhere except
in our hearts and in infinity?" we had a child.

Gondwana proved elusive. Later Gregory and I fought
about our squares, he saying the scheme conceded
too much to the Nazis,
though Ruth applied it to the Japanese
when the long war flared back up.
Gregory led the Allies into our Eden.
One hundred natives perished because
the Japanese thought they had collaborated.
Sixty thousand Allied soldiers died of malaria.
Decades later *The Chrysanthemum and the Sword* sat,
a self-effacing bomb, on the dusty shelves of grad students.
I outlived Ruth by thirty years, returned to the Sepik twice.
Partnered finally with another who studied its cultures,
I came to embody the modern, ever seeking
that which turned me novice, headless,
then building my language boats,
triangulating my way home,
back to the imperishable stars.

Conjuring Moses

"The sun, from the human point of view (in other words, as it is confused with the notion of noon) is the most elevated conception. It is also the most abstract object, since it is impossible to look at it fixedly at that time of day."—Georges Bataille, "Rotten Sun," 1930

"With her hair blowing over her face she could look directly into the ivory sun.... Her mind began to get quiet and then empty but when the priest raised the monstrance with the Host shining ivory-colored in the center of it, she was thinking of the tent at the fair that had the freak in it. The freak was saying, 'I don't dispute hit. This is the way He wanted me to be.'"—Flannery O'Connor, "A Temple of the Holy Ghost," 1954

"A god ignored is a demon born."—Peter Carroll, *Liber Kaos, The Psychonomicon*, 1992

Freud

On a Vienna street a solar monstrance
threw sunbeams into the professor's eye,
some saint's day, when these benevolent idolaters
paraded their host through Klimt's golden city.
Freud harbored a sort of fondness for Catholicism.
The church had protected him for years.
They had mutual interests, a common focus
on cures by confession, a taste for squirmy details,
that which others avoided. Now this sun disk
transported him to his private mirror universe,
his esoteric study, the swirling questions
that haunted him: What made a Jew a Jew?
Genetics? Culture? the Law? This last gave
him pause. What if the giver of the law
wasn't Jewish, but Egyptian? Although
the eternal god once offered to destroy
Israel, make Moses the father of a new people,
He never said Moses was one of them,
except when they erred, once. Moses spoke
of "the Lord, the God of *your* fathers."
Michelangelo had made Moses horned, not,
as the Christian simpletons thought, meaning him
a devil, but attuned: survivor of an ancient alien race,
a powerful being like the Greek gods, Sol Invictus,
—or like Ikhnaton himself. Backed by the unpopular
god of reason and unreason who must be first,
who could be represented only as the sun's rays,
the sect priest in exile, looking for a people.
The Torah had him horned but also radiant,
his face glowing so that he required a veil,
a troubling creature between god and human.

Crosses and stars take precedence among the oldest
human signs—a symbol of the divine presence,
coeval with the species itself as far as we know.
Over syncretic millennia since the time of Moses,
the day star's rays re-emerged in art, surrounding saints,
framing the new god's mother, emitted from
the sacred heart of Jesus. Over time this new heretic
offshoot hit upon the monstrance as a substitute
for the lettered tablets. What use to show words
to an illiterate people? No, much better
if the tablet were a translucent piece of bread
surrounded by a sun disk, carried through the streets
in the old pagan way. This message
the people could understand:
food, circumscribed by the golden god.
That they would kill for. The masses always loved
their volcanos, their war gods, hungry for blood.
Taboo to eat it, but permitted to spill, within measure.
The icon spread through political language,
rising up through socialist posters and broadsides.
The question haunted the merchant's son.
Long before the Jewish self-hater king began his purges,
raising his black sun lifted from Hindus over Europe,
Freud read every new study of Ikhnaten,
collected over 600 Egyptian artifacts. Germans
had written about Moses for more than a century.
Sellin felt certain the Jews hadn't killed Jesus,
but they had offed Moses. After which, Freud thought,
like other primal murderers, they felt guilty.
He introduced the idea tentatively in *Totem and Taboo*,
then kept going, like a tongue probing a sore tooth.

At first Freud was magnetized to the subject
through his own alienation. A believer

in race, wistful about being excluded
from all that was German, though he called
himself "Mediterranean." What if he could prove
it had all been a lie? Would this new Pharaoh
take them back? But he couldn't. Then he worried
over the future of psychoanalysis, whether
it might wash under, having been classified
as "Jewish science" because so many followers
were from his race. If only Jung hadn't rebelled
over his Gnostic nonsense, he would have
been the perfect German face of what Freud,
in letters, often called *psi*, his Teutonic crown prince.
Of all the betrayals, this child's stung the most.
It looked as if the English would save the movement
now, led by the little Celtic pervert and other anti-Semites.
A conspiracy was underway already: his Nazi friends
had named their prices to look aside or whatever would
be their part. Jones' Jewish wife could translate his book.
To wash up in London, dependent,
like Marx. What an end.
The depth of his exile kept growing.
Sometimes he wondered what could redeem all this.
The cancer, entrenched, had spread to his head.
Soon enough he would be gone anyway.
But he couldn't leave his Mosaic
perseverations in their hands and not be there.
Like Moses, he had received his death sentence.
An image came back to him from 1909, meeting
William James. In an attack of the near-final angina,
the American had brushed aside his concerns; instead
asked Freud to carry his bag and walk ahead.

Jump at the Sun

Half a world away, on a houseboat in Florida,
Zora had been reading Gerald Massey. She saw
Moses ascending bodily like Enoch or Elijah,
not a prophet but a magician,
a repository of the wisdom of Africa,
a guardian of the doors of perception.
Massey thought the ancient compilers of Torah
had recycled Egyptian myth, but, unable
to understand hieroglyphs, misread.
The imported errors turned out
to have their own magical powers.
Magic and error, intrinsically linked:
magic inheres in sound, hidden from
the commons in texts. Only insiders
to traditions know the proper accents.
It wasn't knowing the word *abracadabra*
or some such, but knowing how to say it.
The corruption carried yet a strong power
of making, the lessons of Enoch:
the broken pieces still sing.

The invisible god was a hard master, all found.
His first claim on Akhenaten had been his posterity
as a king. The sun god is heartless, Zora noted.
It would have been hard to get workers to follow him.
Then He took the pharaoh's name, sent haters out to chip his
hieroglyph off the records and replace it with "heretic."
He would not let him rest in his tomb.
No burial shrines for his followers. A jealous
and violent ruler, this god kept devils on staff,
sent plagues and invading armies against his chosen
to remind them of his greatness and mercy.

The people went ahead to their destiny,
but Moses their leader was lost in the desert.
To the sun god belongs reason and madness.

At the onset of the Holocaust,
a wave of bad magic against the Jews
raged so strongly that even the foremost
figures of Judaic culture and learning
experienced racial doubt: modernists
had already laid the ground, clearing
the way for new master narratives to arise.
What if it had all been a misunderstood
rehash of Egyptian astronomic myths?
The secrets of fundamental water, uncreated *nun*,
skipped over in the Hebrew Genesis.
But the lesson of Moses, as Kafka reflected,
lay in his very humanity: even in error,
we can still be blessed. He never
wanted the job or sought fame. He had been
written out of the books once already.
He hid in the desert with Jethro/Reuel's magicians
for decades. Massey thought the story still golden.
Moses had to break the tablets to prevent
confusion between the image and the idea.
The more learned he became, the more literate
in the language of birds and lizards, the harder
his task: how to represent a god who cannot be named
or depicted, to persuade a people
to raise his power, enact his rule?
Rituals, bodies of law, and everyday habits
build this house of light.
Zora nodded. One letter's difference
between law and lwa.

People of the Sun

Giving back heads taken by time, anti-iconoclast,
a god-keeper of Mexico painted her reading
of Freud's last book near the end of the second world war.
She had planned to be a doctor. A second birth
on September 17, 1925 put paid to that fantasy.
Lying naked in the street, she had waited
for La Pelona, but instead an Aztec sun drew
her eye to the trickster's joke, her broken body coated
in gold dust. Twenty years on, she well knew
the ways of the skeleton, uncredentialed,
but expert on body matters, health and decay.
Only Freud had more surgeries than she: 34 to her 32.
In pain and in paint, inspired by Freud's thesis,
she figured forth the polymorphous lineage of
the invisible god: beginning with the sun
and his creatures, the larger ancestry
of light and dark (like Nietzsche, she knew
"the night is also a sun"); reptiles,
monkeys, insects among the array.
Framing the scene, sexual reproduction
itself as a kind of progenitor, nodding to
the ghost of Amon, the hidden god conjoined
to the sun's rays, then the infant Moses,
the abandoned child, future left to chance,
with his third eye, at the center. On the margins
the sideways sibling logic, the metonymy,
the synecdoche of monotheism, long ripples
on a big pool. Unflinching, heterodox,
she placed the pyramid builders of both worlds
in parallel: Egyptians and Aztecs, as well as
the secular humanists and destroyers
of modernity: Marx and Adam Smith;

Napoleon and Hitler ("the lost child,"
she called him, the anti-Moses), Freud himself,
of course, the Soviets and Gandhi-ji
with Lao-Tse and the Buddha. Tracing
the spread of an idea through time, she pointed
the sun's fingers to Jesus and the buried skeleton.
Unrepentant daughter of the earth, Kahlo knew:
these wizards' wars are merely weather.
Tears rain down over the open-eyed child;
Nefertiti and Akhenaten watch on either side.
She called it Moses, the nucleus of creation.

El Norte

Moses' DMT may have come from acacia, the wood
he used for the ark. Oppenheimer's drugs of choice
had always been nicotine and adrenaline. More of a
prophet than a lawgiver, good at predictions—
he understood speed. The government titled him
Coordinator of Rapid Rupture. By the thirties
he had leaped ahead of his fellows
with his stellar physics and bad arithmetic
to study gravitational collapse, but left
his parlor communist CalTech friends behind,
entered a high-stakes race against German light wizards
who had been his friends at Göttingen. His darting mind
veered away from the predicted black holes, back
to his other love, the sun-lit desert. When the luminaries
came into New Mexico's mountains to work in seclusion,
the Allemagne were well established in the lead. As Aron
observed, it could so easily have been their century.

A British experiment with gold had set Heisenberg on his
course soon after Freud's first visit to Moses in Rome,
about the same time Einstein predicted gravitational
deflection of starlight as it passed near the sun.
The Eddington pair verified it in an eclipse of 1919.
In the teens and twenties the German physicists
were killing it with their radiation analysis;
Hess took ionization readers up in a balloon
during an eclipse, wagering his own life in the test
to measure air's conductivity, an old school alchemist.
Chadwick's discovery of the neutron nearly
completed the map of the sub-atom, the cellular sun
hidden in all things. Chemists had begun
studying chain reactions, and by the time

the French discovered the advantage of uranium
and patented the idea of an atomic bomb,
Germans had already divided the nucleus,
found the energy produced in a chain
of newly created particles. But then, in the mid-
thirties, Hitler decreed the great purge:
1150 Jewish scientists fled or were pushed out;
all told, by 1934 Göttingen seemed dead,
a hollow name, the children of God gone.

The mountain top is a dangerous place.
As the hideous light bloomed in the desert,
Oppenheimer first felt relief; in the next breath,
it seemed, he saw himself in universal scale, as if
he had ingested an entheogen. The eternal god
had not meant this, when He directed Jews to be
"a light unto the nations." Only esoteric studies
could make sense of his fate. The secret police
had kept a close eye on him at Los Alamos; word
of his repentance spread like fire. He fell
afoul of orthodoxy, began to lose his name.
The balding new Pharaoh, he of the finger-snap
decision-making, a son of "show me," saw him once
to hand off an obligatory medal, then told his aide,
"I don't want to see that son of a bitch in this office ever again."
Then came the iconoclasts, chipping away at his repute.
They said he couldn't read material he had written.
He ran out of people to throw under the bus,
named names to no avail, got sent to Princeton
to succeed Einstein, spent the rest of life
teaching ethics to scientists, but it was no good.
His error had broken the world, had a power of its own.
The week before Kennedy was killed, Opje
joked with Thomas Kuhn that the J at the start

of his name meant "nothing," an empty variable.
In luxury and loneliness, like Freud, he died
of throat cancer. His ashes were dropped in the sea.

Moses, Man of the Mountain

When almighty God speaks to you
out of a bush that burns but is not
consumed, forget it:
"your" life is over.
Sometimes he felt he had been born
without story. In his lifetime suffering
the pangs and fear of birth again and again,
always coming back to face
that emptiness, the place
where darkness and light
have always been one.
Even his name was empty:
the child, the son: who names
an innocent such a thing?
Where was the father whose glory
he should have preserved?
But the princess shook her head,
silent and androgynous
as the Sphinx, and so
he remained simply Moses.
Having followed the Heretic
into the desert to build
the new city and forfeited
position among the royals,
when it all came to nothing
and he became a murderer,
he believed he had
nothing else to lose.
Looking back on his innocence
years later made him laugh.
So many losses yet awaited.

He turned his back on Amarna's
builders and fled, washed up
among the desert magicians,
who sent him to breathe
strange fumes at the burning bush.
There their faceless god of becoming,
Eh Yeh Asher Eh Yeh,
remade him into a giver of law,
the temporary savior of a perpetually
doubting and ingrate people.
The desert fathers taught him
snake magic, introduced him
to the god molecule, made him
a keeper of Africa's darkest
secrets, laughed at his protests
about his uncircumcised lips
and the limits of language,
then sent him back to Egypt
to work greater feats.
It's easy to be enlightened
within yourself. Fasting
forty days on a volcano
is nothing. But can you
bring a people into the desert,
convince them to leave
the devil they know and live
there being reprogrammed
and eating mushrooms
for forty years? A jubilee?
Can you extract a people
from an enslaved rabble?
Now that's alchemy.

He didn't want to reenact
the trials of Akhenaten.
He knew full well the builders
never stopped worshipping
the old gods, undermining
the sun-washed city as fast as it rose.
People do love their idols,
their slave civilizations—
even when they are the slaves—
the cruelty of sacrifice
and captivity, having
enemies and gods "out there."
Only plagues and genocide
can pry them away from
the trash they treasure,
convince them to begin again.
He even had to do it to them,
let a generation die off
to start fresh, and another time
unleashing the Urim against
those who got too friendly
with the natives at Moab.

He wondered at odd moments
what it might have been like if,
after that day at the well in Midian,
he had become a simple shepherd.
What if he and Tzipporah had kept
a flock and raised their boys,
eating and sleeping, going out
at night to watch the stars,
with never a thought beyond

daily life, their routine between
the well and the mountain.
The life of the patriarchs was good.
He was no Abraham, had no innate passion
for destroying idols. When he left the city
he would never have returned,
had it been up to him. But that
was just Orientalism. In truth, Reuel
had pulled him into turf wars
from the start. These desert tribes
were never without guile; the very thought
proved fatal to their enemies.
He waged genocidal war against them,
in the end, but it didn't save him.
Midianite wizards survived the slaughter,
hiding in their desert caves, found ways
to collude with the Levites who chafed
under his rule, picked off or turned
his loyal helpers one by one. Later,
they prettied it up with a tale about how
he had insufficiently given the glory to God
when he struck water out of the ground with his rod
in the wilderness of Tzin. To sweeten the loss,
they made up a tale that he had been
an Israelite baby saved from a genocide
through trickery, not some princess' bastard,
fathered God knows where. The sun shone
alike on the glory and the murders,
showing favor to all and none, as is its way.

Building the Diamond Body

What's Bugging Her

At the near-empty train station
a small sting on the face:
only a month back would have sent her
into panic, guilt, and shame.
Today she rubs it and forgets.
The sensation is the same.
No narrative freight today,
to derail her into crazytown.
She examines her experience
like a bug under a microscope,
remembers a day at the onset of madness.
In the bath house, she lay exhausted
below an infrared lamp, naked and wet.
Eyes closed against the light, she felt
water trickle down her skin and knew
it felt the same as the buggy creeps.
A different story kept her above
the drain, kept her sure and solid.
But she could not hold it, lost her grip.

At some point bugs entered the house,
real and seen by others. She thinks she had
the world's easiest change of life, but,
it could be, the crawling skin was, as well,
one last symptom, one last middle finger
raised to the sky by departing hormones
scorching their path back to hell,
psychotic to the end. Also: eczema,
real, place in sequence unknown.
This and/or the real bugs, all.
Three in combination, two. Then one.
A fourth variable: a commonplace of siege,

the deteriorating mind, breaking down,
pulling itself up. She began
to fear the slightest itch, a mite jumpy,
Aaron might say. Any speck, a hair falling
on her arm, a pill in the seam of a garment,
a sensation of dry and burning skin,
wool or cat hair, chafing clothes, a minute
swelling capillary, unreachable,
just under the shoulder blade, none
ever again itself alone, but drove
a freighted train of story and duty,
seemingly brakeless. Dead skin cells
on the computer screen, cat dander, even
common dust spiraled her
into frenzies of daily cleaning.

Everywhere she saw and felt more. This,
the real bugs, skin irritation, hormonal effects,
all, any two or three combined, or one. Impossible to see
when it changed, gradations and borders.
The senses no longer to be trusted.
Nothing to do but give in, collapse.
At the end of the tunnel she found herself
irrationally lucid, hoping,
gaining purchase, feeling better.
Say it five ways, like old films about AI:
PERHAPS I am only crazy.
Perhaps **I** am only crazy.
Perhaps I AM only crazy.
Perhaps I am ONLY crazy.
Perhaps I am only CRAZY.
And so she grew well.

Broken Landings

No one is home
when the mind's eye opens.
Maybe a bird outside the window:
chickadee, chickadee, chick chick chick.
A small black presence
uncurls warmth from the spine.
Residual aches of grinding teeth,
a crick spread from neck
to shoulders, a thought:
find money for rolfing.
I miss touch, solvency,
days not blue.
On the ceiling the sun
makes three small kites.
I remember my open heart.
It smiles at me from dreams,
reminds me to breathe.

Ancestors Come to Greet Us

Her name was Pat. Of course it was.
Hair dyed red. An old rock-n-roller, deaf,
couldn't speak after throat cancer,
peripheral neuropathy and
moved with a walker, recovering
alcoholic. She could see with glasses,
had maybe 50% manual dexterity,
suffered ladies' issues. I mean,
she had burned that mother down.
She was the original disco inferno.
An embodied Tower of sidewalk Tarot,
an ancient yogi, queenly in her ashes.
I knew her as soon as we met.
She was in my bones, with the face
of a Dulac mermaid, a shrunken fairy,
my wee grannie of a millennium ago
wearing a black t-shirt that said
NO BACK STAGE PASSES.
We freaked the passersby on downtown
walks, outwardly telepathic, or
in seeming one-sided talk
as I read her shriveled lips.
Once a homeless man sprang at us,
calling her "mother" with personal
menace, as if settling accounts from
ancient forests, rocked the square
with blasted accusations:
"WITCHES! WITCHES!"
He brandished his proof, torn-out *Vogue*
pages, images of Giselle Bundchen.
She was afraid. I, angry and terse:
"we are not your enemies."

The words carried reason, yet,
involuntary, my body squared up, ready
for the fights that brought Mama to life.
Before I could feed that fire,
two gentlemen flanked us,
one black and one white: "We would like
to walk you ladies to your car, if you don't mind."
We didn't. I packed her into the truck grimly, clicked
the belt into place across her trembling frame, hefted
her collapsed walker into the back, reflecting:
I hadn't beaten anyone with it, a victory
over my genes. I nodded to the gents, got in,
and drove away. We never spoke of it again.

Building the Diamond Body

Formerly her skin had been firm as apples.
Now she looked in the mirror and saw sags,
pockets of disuse. Adjusting her eyes,
she observed the skull behind the face.
She was a scientist. She knew what came next.
Impervious, cancer had raced through her upper torso,
unfazed by radium, phosphorous cocktails, or other fires,
then leaping from soft tissues to bone.
Nothing was left to protect her heart. But no matter.
The table had always appeared in the wilderness.
Terrain would be different. Already was.
She took in her caving body. Vitality had drained.
Small sips of life came in music, or nightly
forays outside to see the stars, if she felt strong, and—
maybe—one last feast awaited before death's kingdom.

For years she haunted the tide pools
of beaches and barrier islands along the East coast.
Rachel Carson sightings had been reported,
as if she were a rare migrating bird.
She stood for hours in frigid waters,
observing and appreciating fellow transients.
Male companions carried her away in their arms,
legs insensate, all command of nerves lost.
Becoming mermaid: her first time on a submarine,
the crew tried to frighten the two ladies.
She pretended not to notice the night noise.
The same with real demons—cutting dead
disappointment, poverty, loss, internal whispers that
perhaps she was unequal
to being a parent—then adopting her niece's child,
and ten years' keeping of a secret love.

Unafraid of being visible, she balanced
government reports with love letters to the great chain
of being, known as a poet of the sea. *The New Yorker*
carried her calls for kinship throughout the world, and
responses began to land at her home and office.
Readers made her a confessor. She tried to answer them all.
When alarms began to stream in,
tales of death sprayed from the skies,
of silenced songbirds and dead barn cats
across entire counties, like Jesus, she weakly prayed
for the cup to be taken from her. Even Dorothy said,
please don't do this.

But just as she had loved larval eels
and other slitherers of the ocean floor, just as
she went out of her way to save a trapped firefly
or to console her love, letting butterfly migrations
animate how their story would come to make sense
in the future, so she became the guardian of the insects.
Reminding the Big Everything Complex that they were not all.
No, in truth minute in the cosmic order, design
having spawned even mosquitoes, carpet-eating moths
so hated by Alice B. Toklas, biblical proportions of
locusts and grasshoppers, the multivariate so-called pests.
Insisting that in harming the least, the powers
sinned against all, not letting it go.

Hate mail began to find its way to her.
As she testified to the creep of poisons,
suffusing the food cycle, reaching larger animals,
even humans, never breaking down, lingering in soil,
where there too, according to her,
lives were worth saving, establishment figures saw

she was an infidel. At Cold War's zenith, anyone could
have foretold the default response, the flip side of the old saw
Hentoff said wasn't worth another nickel:
to question DDT's wartime miracle, Miss Carson
must be a Communist. But the FBI closed
that preposterous file pretty fast.

She was a petite woman, wiry,
rather like a bird herself, shoulders frozen forward,
the kyphotic neck of even the outdoorsy who live in
their heads. Never feeling her wings, protecting
the heart that brooded over her unlikely charges,
and determined to finish what Dorothy called
the death book, facing down the critics at every
turn, she went from doctor visits and surgeries
to interviews, radio shows, even TV. Writing full time,
racing the clock, she pulled on a wig after treatments,
painted her face rosy, stuffed her clothes so to seem
hale as ever. Mustn't let Big Chem see its victory
in her body, the mass that tried to elbow her big heart
aside. So she never uttered a word about breast cancer,
never condemned them for her own harms.
She had worn a disguise her whole life, anyway,
this bodhisattva. What was one more?
The wig she called Betty.

After the Ex

In the nectar hour, amid owl song, a dreamer
finds herself flying over rimed prairie,
returning to a town where she used to live,
which is all the towns where she used to live,
searching for the man she loved for so long.
Making her way in the dark, she feels certain
this is the neighborhood. He is close, now.
I can feel it. But, as is always the way,
the path goes sideways, winds through
the landlord's bedroom, where Dick Gregory,
with trippy purple wallpaper, sits up
feeling chatty, watching TV with his daughter.

The dreamer follows the daughter through
the rambling house's turns back on itself,
the doors that will hardly open. No ex
in sight. Instead they meet a cat
who lost its tail to frostbite:
bobbed, imbalanced, pitiful.
The dreamer says, *I'd like to go back out now.*
Is there another way? The guide puts on her hat.
A turn sets the little mermaid's tail chiming
against the lamp's long cylinder; the dreamer
hears the rain, single drops gently falling on the roof,
and a tree, with its own rhythm, brushes the house.
Another turn, and there is St. Lazarus in the window.
He gives her a wink. The tree whispers,
Beloved. Welcome. I have missed you.

Salve, Spider

More like Walt's than Jonathan's, and tiny herself,
she's come to hunt the specks of water bugs
that enter through ungrouted cracks
of an old house in a nice neighborhood.
I've been pouring basil oil into the house,
heading them off her way.
Fearless—when I put my finger into the sink
to keep her from needless drowning, she
hops on board, ready to ride this possible disaster.
Gentle, I shake her away behind the drainpipe.
Dislocation and ephemeral suspension are her jam.
Weightless, still, she has a gravity, this guru.
Willa Cather had it right:
at times we travel fastest by storm.

Sentinel

(for Tracy L. Smith, April 2020)

Perhaps, in another lifetime,
we guarded city gates together,
took shifts in a tower, watched
through the night so the people
could sleep in peace.
This time we are only teachers.
In the plague time spring
the city grows quiet again.
From my ridge on the east side
I listen as the pre-dawn stages
a new symphony: these days
one might wake to hear
thunder rolling long
in the western counties,
maybe as far as the border.
Ears grown numb
to daily jets now pick up
a storm an hour or two out.
To be sure, one tests the edges
of other sounds. A plane, plowing
down toward Earth, has a whine.
A freight train is closer to thunder,
hollow bellies rumbling, ominous.
Single birds
pipe in the darkness.
Trees rustle and brush.
The MARTA train whistles
down its rail like the single car
that rolls through my short cut street
before the traffic builds to a roar.

Miles away the day's first siren
sends its signal looping far above the rest.
Still in darkness, I think of prairie horsemen,
how they could listen to the ground and know
how many riders approached. They say the Earth
has a resonance. I wonder whether, long ago,
before humans became so clamorous,
night watchers like us could hear the stars.

Strange Angels

"Chance is powerful. Let your nets always be cast."—Ovid

1.
That first time she traveled with them, at four,
it had been mosquitoes, probably, on Quentin's boat.
He set her on top of the cabin to let her fly.
Remembering Gnat Island, the ocean bliss,
and then the fever and delirium, sweating
under ceiling fans that spun the room,
feeling lucky, now in Charleston's streets
she soaked up the sun, thanking serendipity
and chance for a work trip here. After
eighteen months walking a friend
to the edge of death, she had some slack
to breathe, to consider ancestral healing.
Many spare hours she sat in the park near the battery
where the war began—now, surely a sign, a heron rookery—
communing with the spirits of place.

Following the Gullah guide from Blue Bicycle,
walking west from the college, she found
Denmark Vesey's houses, no markers. Living on
sushi and caramel apples, quickly bored by King Street,
she haunted the gate-laced byways near the French Quarter
seeking Sophie and the deduced family of Huguenot
Atlantic traders. Never having summoned the courage to face
New Orleans, she thought she could handle this place.
An incorrect assumption. The slave market, she read,
had originally filled the block. The small museum
smelled of dust. She could taste despair, almost touch it.
There had been an ordinance, she read, to stop them
inspecting naked women in the streets because
the white ladies found it offensive.

Nearby she came upon Old Missy's church, and the home
of a merchant Sophie had mentioned by name. That night
three Africans came for her. In red tribal dress,
faces dotted with white, bearing juju, intending her death,
she believed, but she somehow
talked them out of it. Unappeased,
unforgiving, they threw the bags down on the threshold
of her small room at the back of the inn, turned sharply,
and strode away, vanished in the parking lot. Heart pounding,
she sat up in bed. *I'm alive. I'm alive. I'm alive.*
She had to stop this foolishness. It always happened,
like with the schizophrenic at work, the married
philanderers, or the mad among street people,
because she saw them, was unguarded.

2.
Once long ago a watcher flew into her dreams.
He carried her back in time, high into cloudy mountains
to watch ancient peoples roving across Europe.
From his perspective it looked like unending war.
There she'd first heard the words, *Tuatha De' Danann.*
She looked them up when she awoke. Now in the dark
she lay a long time imagining waves of humans
washing up in this port, mostly against their will.
Well, the inn was haunted. She might have guessed.
Ladied up, reporting to the museum, resolute
and well-behaved that evening:
she did not say one weird thing, as over
dinner the artist spoke of Charleston and Beijing,
the legacies and hidden genealogy of cities, wedding
china, who got invited for a seat at the table, freshly
unearthed bodies of the enslaved, ancient poetry,
summoning rituals for dead souls, and art's mirror.
She felt a headache coming on, declined wine and dessert.

Before leaving the area, Skeleton Woman drove out
to see Angel Oak. The old tree was tired of humans.
Its limbs artificially propped and held in place by cables;
people crawled over it like ants, taking selfies.
She stepped back to the edge of the clearing, unwilling parasite.
The very earth seemed worn out. She came away
with illness in her pipes, filled her truck with gas,
retraced the country roads to Atlanta. Maybe it was her;
maybe she walked the edge too long with her dying friend.
Maybe it was too soon, or too late. She felt jetlagged,
bottomless, but not like the freed souls in Jen's painting,
who rose over the swamps, departing the Holy City.

3.
Later that summer, on the trail of Benedict and Mead,
she rode into Poughkeepsie on the train. Pushing through
a research trip, she had to face facts: Chinese ghosts,
traveling with the artist, had attached themselves. Singing
incessantly, often keeping her up all night, they revealed
the engine room, ancient tropes that underslung
street opera and higher arts. They wanted her to know
Cinderella was a prisoner of war, a hapless nameless hostage
whose body was a treaty, a currency of shifting value,
who tried to slip her life between clashing stories.
Sometimes she became the mother of a nation—
more often only a victim—but in a few lifetimes a world purifier,
self-immolating between the warring tribes. These spirits
traced for her the silk road roots of Pan's wild fairy children,
how China and Ireland named them the same word, cognate
with Sanskrit: the *siddhe*, which to the Greeks became
scythe or *Scythians*. The recurring raids on the steppes,
the transcending beauty of the grasslands springing up
in the fecund wakes of glaciers, complicated alliances
of harem life, and the deceit and magic of ancient courts:

not wanting to miss a crumb, she consumed their sweets,
forgoing sleep after days in the archives to listen to their tales.

A sharp prick mid-back in the shower marked the start of it;
at first she'd thought she picked up a tick. Energy sieved
from her like water, but still she barreled along.
Maybe the welts around her ribs were flea bites? No,
shingles: ghosts and angels might be compared to vampires.
These were very old. They promised oceans of wisdom,
a millennium of literature and culture, a new world.
She wanted to spend every moment in thrall to them,
to join them outside of time. Giving up all vanity,
she burned through reserves, resigned to growing old.
Working mornings, then home at lunch, she went to bed.
Usually she could start again. Sometimes twice.
Exercise ended. Acupuncture, gong baths, elderberry
everything. One advanced yoga training. Megadoses of B12.
Vertigo and Epleys. She ate whatever she wanted, slept
when able. Job one was survival. Bras and deodorant
hurt her, so she quit them, wore thick cotton jackets.

4.
She was beginning to understand a little Mandarin
when, at term's end, she treated herself to more research.
On the silver line in DC she picked up another bug.
At first she shrugged it off as a minor annoyance,
a recurring feature of the city, always some Capitol crud;
Archival work, too, entailed sniffles of some variety.
In tears and irritation she found the Benedict letters
at last, interred with Mead's as if to make up
for the faithless, lying decades. As the cache of secrets
spilled, in the fight to capture it Skeleton Woman
felt her desire for life raging back. Dust flew
as she sped through boxes, folders, papers. Slowly an image

came into focus, other storylines spreading to New Mexico;
at night on the internet she followed the glowing web
to Oppenheimer, a human spider at the center.

At home another story emerged: flu, the worst ever.
The astrologer who spoke of sideways elevators
had it right. On one side she slid from the Boas Circle
into the Los Alamos group. On the other she lay confined
to her bed, fighting to breathe for three weeks,
among the avant-garde of a coming pandemic. She wrote
the FBI, requested Ruth Benedict's file. They denied
having one. The bastards, she fumed to her children.
I know they're lying. Sent her awareness into breath.
Drank citrus, tea, honey, whiskey, miso.
Gallons of water. Her lower pipes, at least, had fully healed.
She read Freud for fun. Mostly she coughed.
The nerve pain from shingles still ached, snaking
through the body, around the lung, under the heart.
The exact spot where her friend's cancer exploded.
Was this the end of a curse on her *nadis*? Had she undone
granthis? She had no spiritual cultivation left.
Was this what ancestral healing meant? Dropping baggage,
starting fresh like a baby, with no strength. Every morning
she welcomed the pain like Moses in the sun,
breathing into it: *I'm alive. I'm alive. I'm alive.*

Young William James

"Inveterately indecisive, James was possessed of a character and mind so
wide open that he was almost unable to believe in anything."
—Colin Koopman

Riddled, a man full of holes, enfleshing
all the virtues and vices of his age:
the young man in shades
with the mud-rotted hems, standing for
a portrait in 1865, saved by a cheerful refusal
to care about yesterday's self,
a corrective to the "tedious egoism" needed
to keep himself alive amid virulent ringworm,
mouthfuls of biting flies, and so many mosquito
varieties he grew able to distinguish their bites.
Counting fish, he heard tales of termite mounds
as large as England. Monks had sued them in court.
In his hammock he longed for a nasty winter's day.

Death's omnipresence summoned a constant
struggle to make a difference. He first saw it when
he couldn't see, after smallpox in Brazil.
There Agassiz, a genial racist, taught him the ways
Darwin was wrong and right. Failing next
at art, he then immersed in the ferment of medicine.
Later, at German spa towns, grown secret in pain,
James weathered the possible horror of life
without God—his father's one support.
Son of a devastated theologian, enrolled in
and removed from more schools than most knew existed,
like Peirce, he fought his own demons, and agreed:
Puritan bogeys might offer a kind of salvation.

Befriending chance, embracing doubt, godfather
to Sidis and all those moderns whose blasted beliefs
hung in shreds, useless as his pants from the expedition—
a doctor unable to heal himself, and, a sceptic of
all teachers, relentlessly learning; he arrived
as a teacher of medicine. In the crucible of doubt,
they founded a school of philosophy, asking:
what if our stories only matter when useful? and don't
the evils of violent dogmatism outweigh
those of imagining a godless universe?
If you stare at the photograph long enough,
he reveals himself a wizard whose untethered
children now grow numberless as the stars, scattered
through the firmament of internet ethers
surfing the waves of chance and story.

The Cut

I creep away to sit on the rocks at the cut,
feasting my troubled heart with rhythms
of salt air, sea roar, and bird fishing.

Everything glows on St. George, right down
to the shattered refuse and stinking mollusca
thrown up by retreating waters.

The island itself was broken by this canal.
We have almost no knowledge, now,
of what it was like before war consumed it.

Yet at water's edge, the ordinary restored
to universal settings, the ever-present origin
feels always just around the corner:

over-shod feet re-innervated, all the shoulds
of life across the bridge held without effort at bay.
Even my poems seem winged here.

Each time I come harboring a double wish:
that we will survive, and that this place
will outlive us, our zombie hungers.

Stodgy pelicans turn their awkward bodies
graceful, diving in squadron, then a pivot
at the last moment to land feet first.

They ride serenely, the churning
waves no more than a rocking cradle,
lift off instantly, outside of our time.

Notes

"Susu Watari" alludes to the dust sprites in Hayao Miyazaki's 2001 film *Spirited Away*.

"A Doctor Visit" refers to researched events in the life of William Carlos Williams.

"Baby in Baltimore" refers to researched events in the life of Gertrude Stein, who was a student of William James.

"Three Theories of Art" refers to writers W. H. Auden, Max and Crystal Eastman, and Scott Nearing, as well as the art critics Elizabeth Grosz and Rosalind Krauss.

"Dog Days in Santa Fe, 1925" refers to researched and imagined events in the lives of Ruth Benedict and Margaret Mead, Willa Cather and Edith Lewis, with a passing reference to Robert Oppenheimer.

"Bug Relativism" refers to researched events in the life of Zora Neale Hurston, a student of Ruth Benedict.

"Moderns and Mosquitoes" refers to researched events in the lives of Margaret Mead, Reo Fortune, and Gregory Bateson, with a passing reference to Ruth Benedict.

"Freud" refers to researched and imagined events in the life of Sigmund Freud and theories from his 1939 book *Moses and Monotheism*. The Conjuring Moses cycle engages with the theories set forth in that book.

"Jump at the Sun" refers to researched events in the life of Zora Neale Hurston and her studies to write her 1939 book *Moses, Man of the Mountain*.

"People of the Sun" refers to Frida Kahlo's painting, *Moses, the Seed of Creation*, based on her reading of Freud's book.

"El Norte" refers to researched events in the life of Robert Oppenheimer.

"Moses, Man of the Mountain" refers to researched and imagined events in the life of the prophet Moses.

"Building the Diamond Body" refers to researched events in the life of Rachel Carson.

"Young William James" refers to researched events in the life of William James.

About the Author

Hester L. Furey is a poet and literary historian, a specialist in archival research and hidden histories. A native of south Georgia in the United States, she developed a rich sense of appreciation for the absurd from a very young age. Like many Southerners, she is constantly aware of the past in the present and lives in a world populated by the living and the dead. She began writing as a child, inspired by the journalists who investigated the Watergate scandal, her love of encyclopedias, and poetry's alchemical ability to transform personal experience into something of worth. She is the author of *Little Fish: Poems* (2010) and *Skeleton Woman Buys the Ticket* (2019), and the editor of *Dictionary of Literary Biography 345: American Radical and Reform Writers, Second Series*. She currently resides in Atlanta.

www.ingramcontent.com/pod-product-compliance
Lightning Source LLC
Chambersburg PA
CBHW050226100526
44585CB00017BA/2067